PIANO FOR BEGINNERS
LEARN TO PLAY
CHRISTMAS CAROLS

THE ULTIMATE BEGINNER PIANO SONGBOOK
FOR KIDS WITH LESSONS ON READING NOTES
AND 50 BELOVED SONGS

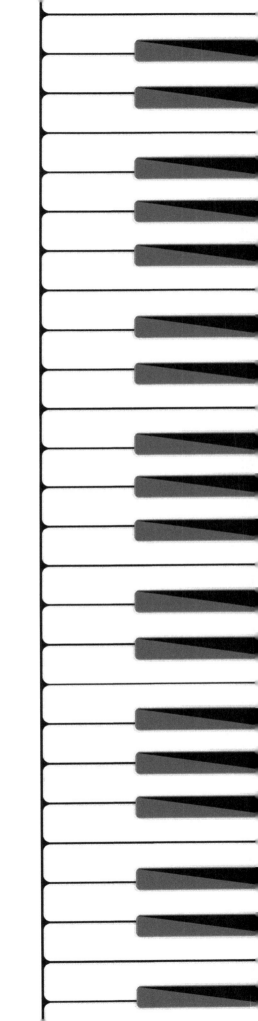

Producer & International Distributor
eBookPro Publishing
www.ebook-pro.com

Piano for Beginners - Learn to Play Christmas Carols
Piano Made Easy Press

Transcribed by Seyapianist

Contact: agency@ebook-pro.com

CONTENTS

INTRODUCTION

Welcome to your first Christmas Carols piano book!

With **30** seasonal and festive songs accompanied by an introductory lesson on the basics of reading notes and divided into three difficulty levels with music lessons throughout, you will be ready for musical Christmas celebrations in no time.

All you will need in addition to this book is a piano or keyboard and some time to practice. Remember – practice makes perfect, and the wide range of songs in this collection will make practicing a true pleasure.

HOW TO USE THIS BOOK

First, read the Get to Know Your Piano section on pages 12-19.

This short guide will teach you the fundamentals of reading notes and playing with your right hand, after which, and with a little practice, any beginning musician will be able to read and play all the music in **Level 1** of this book.

Once you have practiced the songs in Level 1 and feel comfortable learning something new, go on to the second lesson on page 29. This will teach you how to play using both hands – and open up a whole new collection of carols to play.

Once you've perfected Level 2 and want to learn something more, go on over to lesson three on page 52. Here, you will find yet more neat tips and tricks to advance your playing skills and open up the next and final level in this book – **Level 3.**

Don't forget, you can always go back and play earlier songs, even if you've already learned more advanced ones!

SPECIAL VIDEO / AUDIO FEATURE

Learning from a book can be challenging – and sometimes audio and visual aids can help. That is why we've included a special feature in this beginner piano book.

You will notice that every piece of music is accompanied by a QR code adjacent to the title.

Scan the QR code to access a video of that very song being played on piano, where you can hear exactly what the music should sound like and see precisely how to play each note.

Slow the video down or speed it up, skip forward and pause at your convenience – whatever helps you master the tune.

Level 1

GET TO KNOW YOUR PIANO

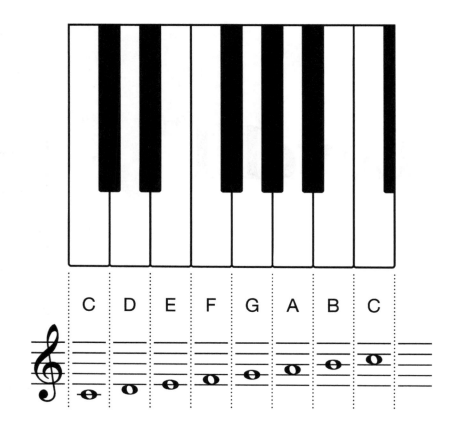

RECOGNIZING KEYS

A piano is made up of **keys**, each of which makes a different sound — called a **note**.

A piano has white keys and black keys — we call the white ones by their letters, from A-G — just like you can see in the picture.

You will notice that the black keys come in groups — first two, then three, and so on.

Look at your piano — and put your finger on the C note. You will recognize it as the white key immediately on the left of the group of two black keys. You will notice that there are several different C keys on your keyboard — we'll always start with the one closest to the middle.

From there, going to your right, play each white note, one at a time — C, D, E, F, G, A, B — just like in the picture.

The more you practice, the easier it will be to recognize the notes — but for now, just remember where the C key is, and work from there!

READING MUSIC

Now, look at the five lines with the swirly symbol on the left. This is a **Treble Clef** 𝄞 which indicates the beginning of a new line of music.

Musical notes are drawn on and between the lines, going from left to right, and now we will learn how to recognize them.

Find the **C note** on your piano again like we learned and look at how it looks on the lines. It is the only note with a line through it — and that is how we will remember it.

From there, the notes go higher up along the lines — with every consecutive note going up one half-line.

So after C comes D, which sits just below the first line. Next is E, which sits right on the middle of the first line — and so on.

The first few times you play, look back at the drawing to remind yourself which note goes where. Once you've practiced a few songs, you should remember them by heart more easily.

UNDERSTANDING NOTE LENGTHS

You will notice that some music notes are black, others are white, some have lines and some only ovals, and others are connected together with beams. All of these things help us understand how long we should keep our finger on the note before we go on to the next one.

This is a **quarter note**. It is the most common and the simplest. Put your finger on one of the piano keys and play a short note – count in your head or out loud to one, and then let go.

This is a **half note**. This note is **twice as long** as a regular note. This time, count to 2 before you let go.

This note is **even longer**, and you'll usually find it at the end of a line or song. It is called a **whole note**. Count to 4 before you move on to the next one.

This note is an 8th note – it is only **half as long** as a quarter note. Press the key once and don't hold your finger on it for long.

Whenever you see a dotted note, like these:

That means you must play for slightly longer than the regular length of the note. So, for example, a dotted quarter note (black with a straight line) will be played slightly longer than a regular quarter note, but less long than a half note.

When you see notes connected with a **beam**, like this:

That means you have to play the notes quickly, one after the other, without pausing in between.

You'll notice that each song has the lyrics written underneath, telling you exactly what to sing for every note.

So, you can also use your knowledge of the songs in the book to help you understand how long each note should be.

RESTS

This symbol is a rest:

It means take a break, and count in your head to one before you play the next note. It is the same length as a quarter note.

This is another rest symbol:

It is a shorter rest – take a break again, but this time, only wait half the time - as long as an 8th note.

If you see two notes connected between them with a tie, like this:

That means you shouldn't stop and lift your finger between both notes, but rather you should play them immediately one after the other.

SHARPS AND FLATS

The black keys on the piano are called **sharps** or **flats**, and they don't have their own names. **D sharp** means the black key to the **right** of D. **D flat** means the black key to the left of D.

A sharp is recognized by this symbol:

While a flat is recognized by this one:

So whenever you see one of these symbols on the music lines next to a note, you'll play the black key that is immediately next to that note – on its right if it is sharp ♯ or its left if it is flat ♭.

Sometimes, throughout the entire song one or two notes will always be sharps or flats. So, instead of putting a sharp or flat symbol next to every single note, we'll put the symbol once at the beginning of every line of music, right next to the Treble Clef, like this:

This is called a **Key Signature.**

In this example, whenever there is a B in the song, we'll make sure to play B flat – the black key immediately to the left of B.

Sometimes, we can have more than one sharp or flat in the song:

In this example, we can see that whenever there is a C or F in the song, we'll play C# or F# - in other words, the black key to the right of C or the black key to the right of F, accordingly.

GETTING STARTED

The numbers above the notes act as guidelines that show you which finger of your right hand to use when playing each note.

1 means use your thumb – and so on until 5, which is your pinky.

Look at this example, from **Jingle Bells**:

The 3, 5, and 1 above the lines help you place your fingers on the keys.

Try it – and sing along!

Remember, playing with the correct fingers is important and will help make sure you are playing the piano in the best possible way!

Later, in Level 2, you will learn how to play music with both hands at the same time. We recommend practicing the simpler songs in Level 1 first, before progressing further.

Congratulations! You've learned how to read music notes.
Now pick out a song and use what you've learned to make some beautiful music!

Deck the Halls

Traditional Christmas Tune

I Saw Three Ships

Traditional Christmas Carol

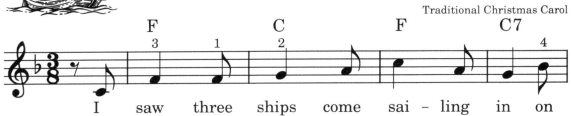

I saw three ships come sai – ling in on

Christ – mas day; on Christ – mas day. I

saw three ships come sai – ling in on

Christ – mas day, in the mor – ning.

Jingle Bells

Traditional Christmas Carol

Jin – gle bells,   jin – gle bells,   jin – gle all the   way!

Oh what fun   it   is to ride in a   one–horse o – pen

sleigh,   hey!   Jin – gle bells,   jin – gle bells,

jin – gle all   the   way!   Oh   what   fun   it

is   to ride in a   one–horse o – pen   sleigh!

Jolly Old St. Nicholas

Traditional Christmas Carol

O Christmas Tree

Traditional Christmas Hymn

Silent Night

Franz Gruber & Joseph Mohr

Si – lent night, ho – ly night.

All is calm, all is bright. 'Round yon

Vir – gin, Mo – ther and Child. Ho – ly

In – fant so ten – der and mild.

Sleep in hea – ven – ly peace –

Sleep – in hea – ven – ly peace.

25

Level 2

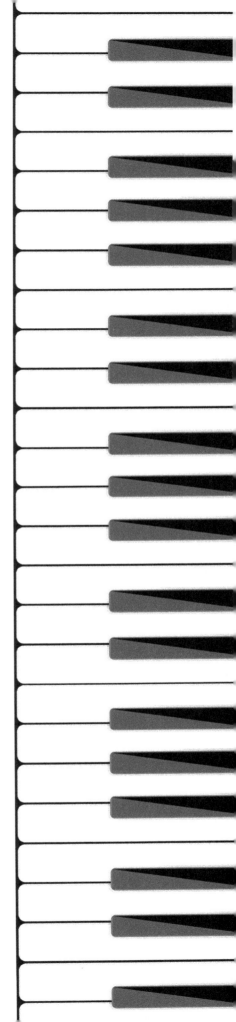

PLAYING WITH BOTH HANDS

Until now, in Level 1, all the music could be played with your right hand only.

In level 2 we will graduate to playing with both hands which will give the songs more life and, of course, increase their level of difficulty.

We recommend beginning by learning how to play a full song with the right hand, and only then incorporating the left hand as well.

In Level 1, we learned about the Treble Clef. That is the marking that indicates the beginning of a new line of music. More accurately, the Treble Clef indicates a line of music meant to be played with the fingers of your right hand.

When we play with both hands, we have two separate lines of music — one on top that begins with a Treble Clef, indicating the right hand, and another on the bottom that begins with a Bass Clef, indicating the left hand.

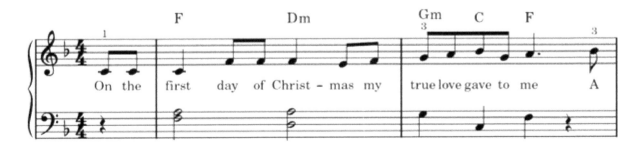

Both lines are meant to be played simultaneously — as you can see, the lyrics pertain to both lines of music, top and bottom.

In Level 1, we learned to recognize keys in Treble Clef (or, the top line of music).

The Bass Clef keys are recognized differently, with the different lines indicating different notes. The order of the notes is still the same – A, B, C, D, E, F, G – but their placing is different.

Take a look at this diagram:

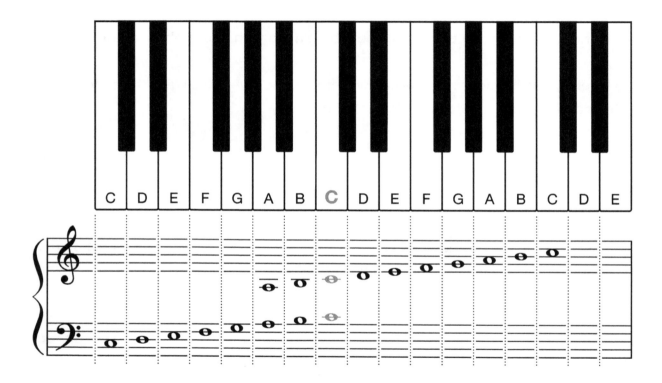

You will notice that the Treble Clef is a direct continuation of the Bass Clef – you will just have to learn a new method of recognizing the keys for your left hand.

A common way of remembering which note is which is by using these mnemonics, with each initial letter indicating where the notes are located on the five lines of the clef:

Every **G**ood **B**oy **D**oes **F**ine (Treble Clef) – the lowest line of music is E, then G, then B and so on.

Good **B**oys **D**o **F**ine **A**lways (Bass Clef) – the lowest line of music is G, then B, then D and so on. In the Bass Clef we will generally use the notes higher up on the lines, as you can see in the diagram.

Come back to this diagram to remind yourself while you're still figuring out the left hand.

Angels We Have Heard On High

Traditional Christmas Hymn

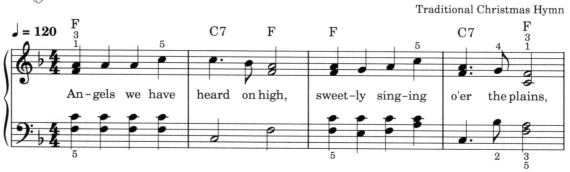

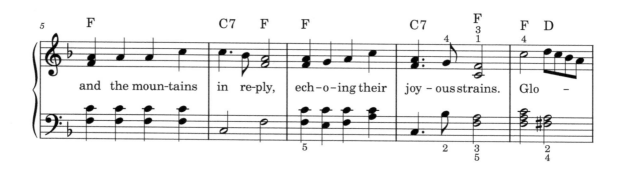

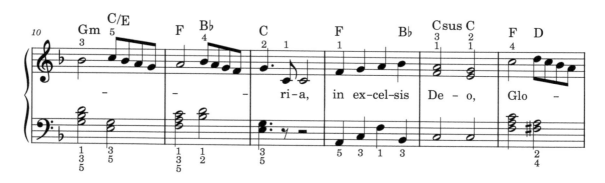

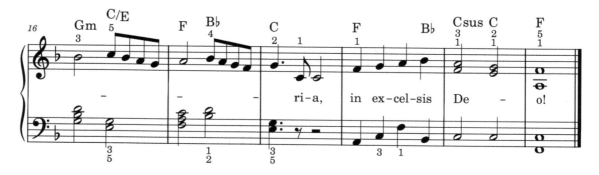

Away in a Manger

Traditional Christmas Hymn

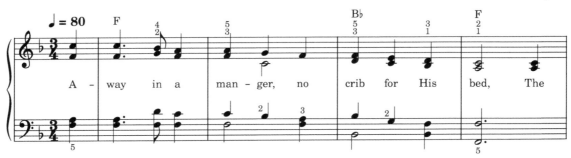

A - way in a man - ger, no crib for His bed, The

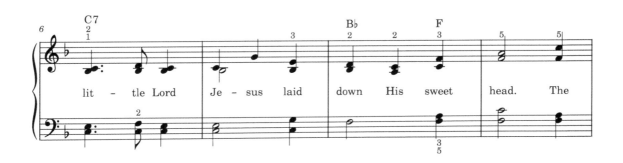

lit - tle Lord Je - sus laid down His sweet head. The

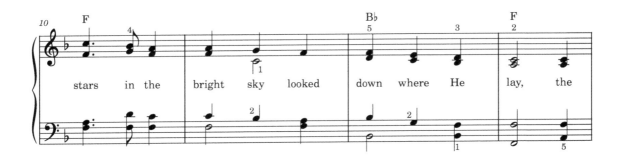

stars in the bright sky looked down where He lay, the

lit - tle Lord Je - sus no cry - ing He makes.

Ding Dong Merrily On High

Traditional Christmas Hymn

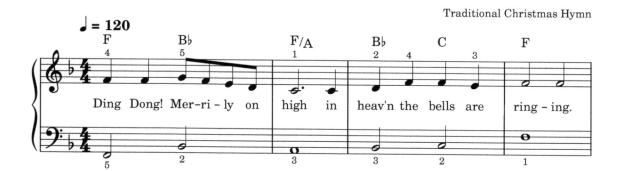

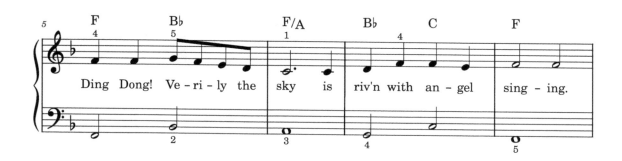

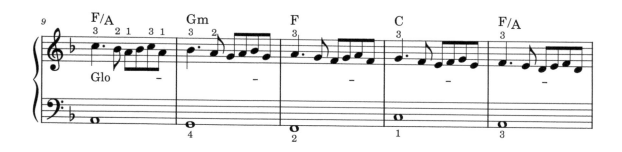

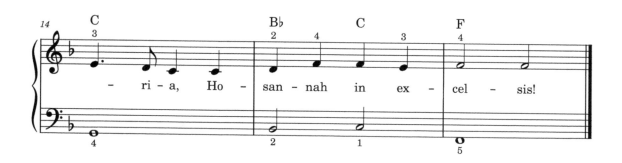

Good King Wenceslas

Traditional Christmas Hymn

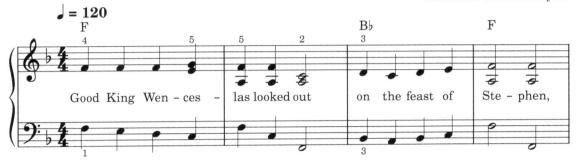

Good King Wen - ces - las looked out on the feast of Ste - phen,

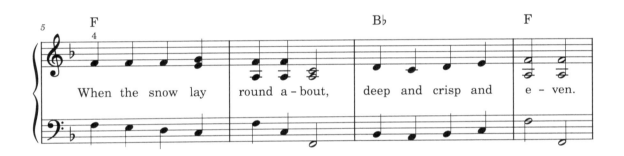

When the snow lay round a - bout, deep and crisp and e - ven.

Bright - ly shone the moon that night, though the frost was cru - el,

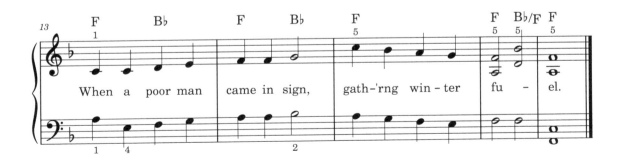

When a poor man came in sign, gath-'rng win - ter fu - el.

Here We Come A-Caroling

Traditional Christmas Hymn

In The Bleak Midwinter

Traditional Christmas Hymn

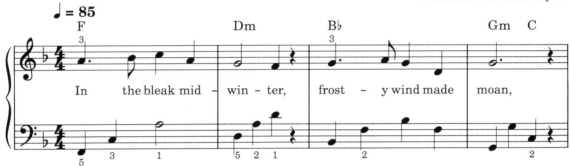

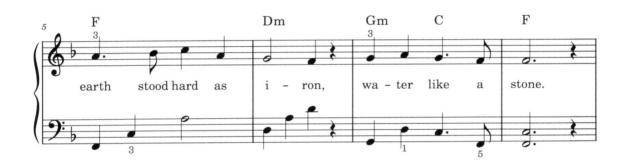

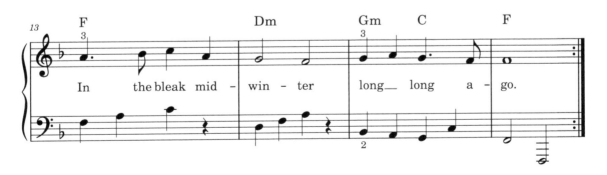

Lo! How a Rose E'er Blooming

Traditional Christmas Hymn

O Come, All Ye Faithful

Traditional Christmas Hymn

O come, all ye faith-ful, joy-ful and tri - um-phant, O come ye, O

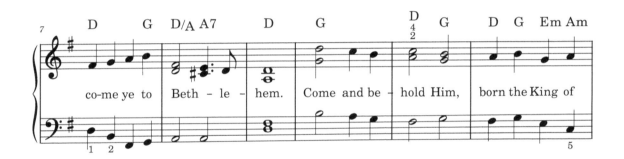

co-me ye to Beth - le - hem. Come and be - hold Him, born the King of

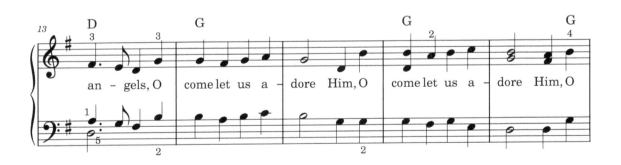

an - gels, O come let us a - dore Him, O come let us a - dore Him, O

come let us a - dore H - im, Chri - st the Lord.

O Come, O Come Emmanuel

Traditional Christmas Hymn

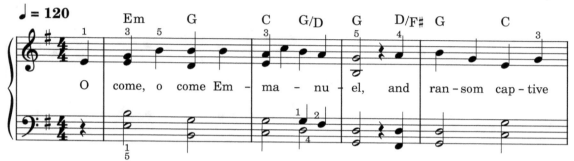

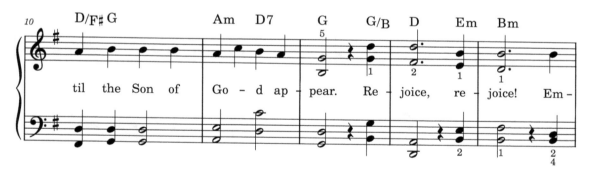

Once In Royal David's City

Traditional Christmas Hymn

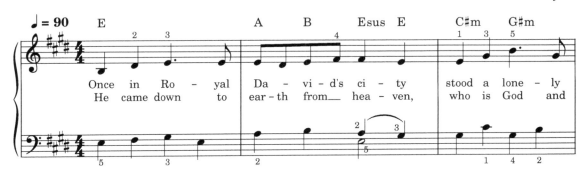

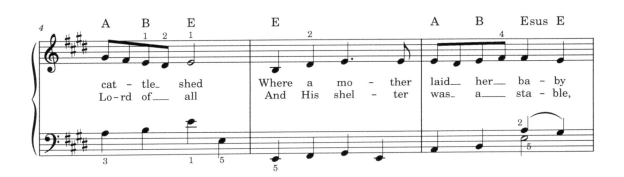

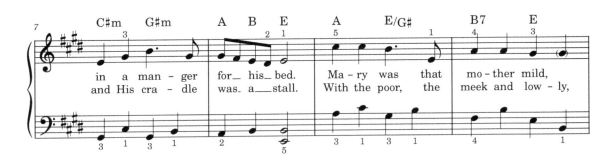

O, Holy Night

Traditional Christmas Hymn

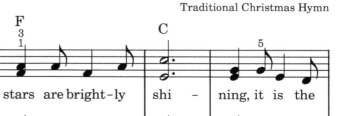

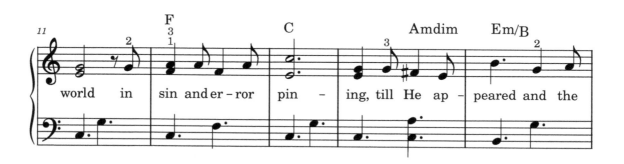

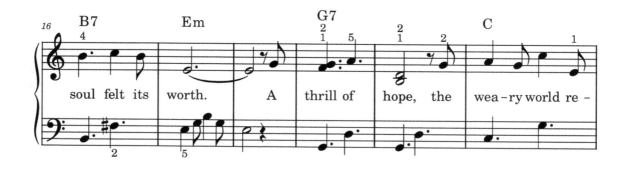

The Coventry Carol

Traditional Christmas Hymn

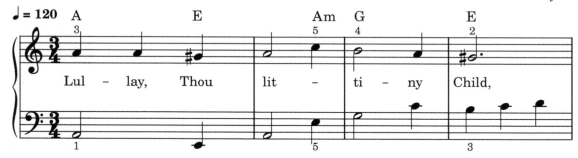

Lul - lay, Thou lit - ti - ny Child,

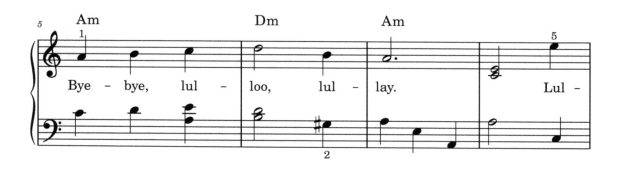

Bye - bye, lul - loo, lul - lay. Lul -

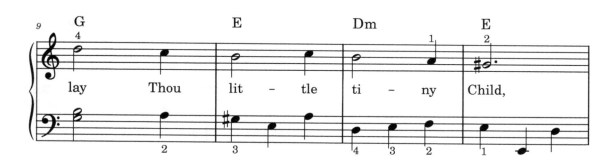

lay Thou lit - tle ti - ny Child,

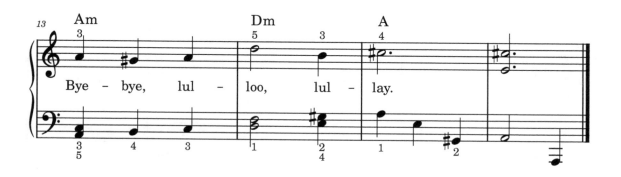

Bye - bye, lul - loo, lul - lay.

The First Noël

Traditional Christmas Hymn

Up On The Housetop

Traditional Christmas Hymn

We Wish You A Merry Christmas

Traditional Christmas Hymn

What Child Is This

Traditional Christmas Hymn

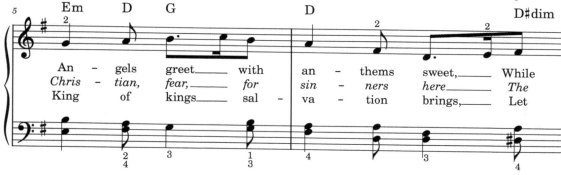

Level 3

MORE NOTATIONS

This symbol is called a **natural**. Remember when we learned about sharps and flats, and key signatures?

Well, a **natural** temporarily cancels out a key signature. In other words, if you have a specific note which is always played sharp, or flat, once you see it with this symbol you must remember to play it in its regular form.

This is a repeat sign. If you see a section of music beginning and ending with repeat brackets, that means this section of the song is meant to be repeated. You will know from the lyrics just how many times the segment should be repeated.

A coda indicates a jump in the music. In the sheet music for Go Tell it On the Mountain, for example, you will see the coda symbol hovering above the final line of music. You can also see, in the middle of the second line of music, the phrase "To Coda". This means that during the final repetition of the music, should you choose to repeat the song, once you reach "To Coda", you must skip the next lines of music and pick up again where you see the coda symbol at the end of the song. This will ensure that the song gets a proper ending.

When you see an accent above or below a note, it means the particular note should be played louder, or stronger, than the other notes. Essentially, the accent does not change the length of the note, but rather its emphasis.

Auld Lang Syne

Traditional Christmas Hymn

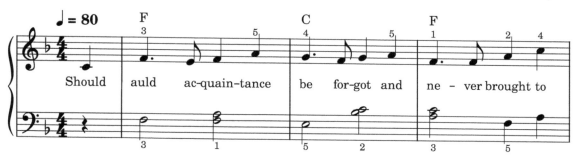

♩ = 80

Should auld ac-quain-tance be for-got and ne – ver brought to

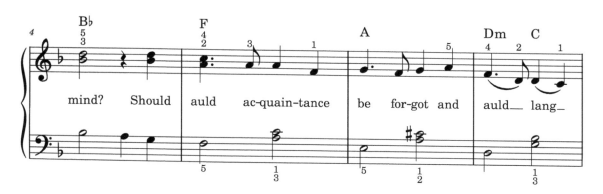

mind? Should auld ac-quain-tance be for-got and auld_ lang_

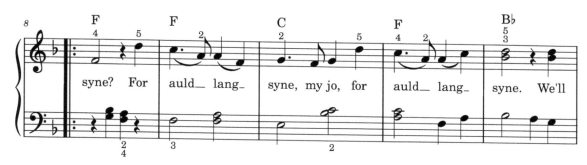

syne? For auld_ lang_ syne, my jo, for auld_ lang_ syne. We'll

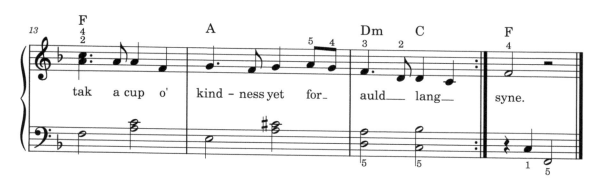

tak a cup o' kind - ness yet for_ auld_ lang_ syne.

Go Tell It On The Mountain

Traditional Christmas Hymn

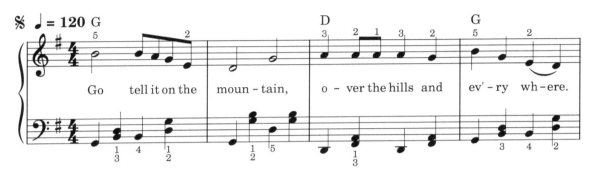

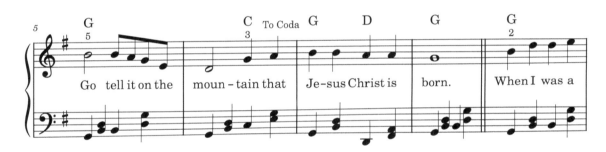

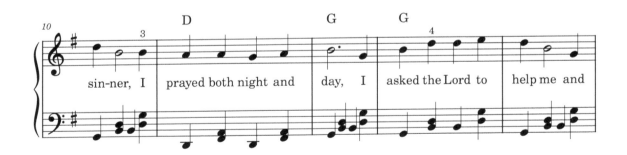

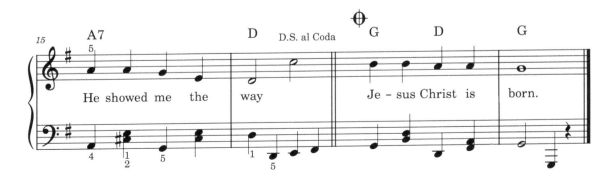

God Rest You, Merry Gentlemen

Traditional Christmas Hymn

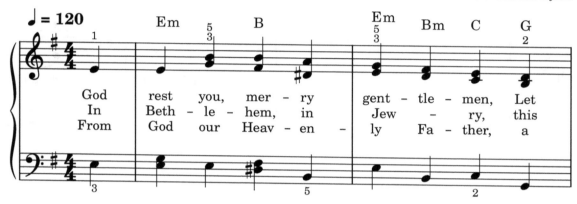

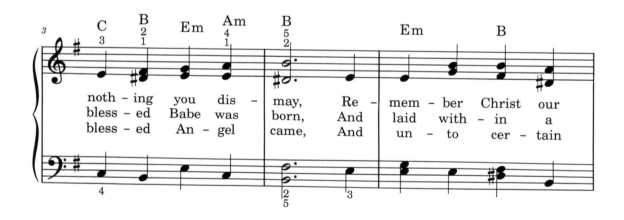

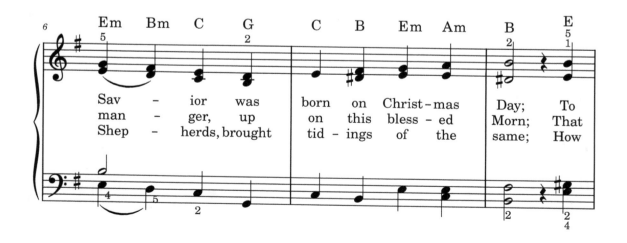

save us all from Sa - tan's pow'r when
which His Moth - er Ma - ry did
that in Beth - le - hem was born the

we were gone a - stray. O tid - ings of
noth - ing take in scorn.
Son of God by Name.

com - fort and joy, com-fort and joy, O

tid - ings of com - fort and joy.

Hark! The Herald Angels Sing

Traditional Christmas Hymn

Joy To The World

Traditional Christmas Hymn

Joy to the world, the Lord is come! Let earth re - ceive her

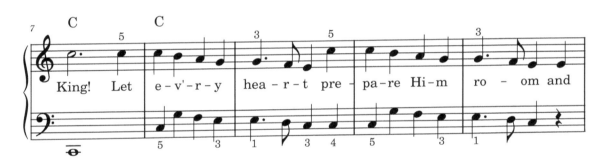

King! Let e - v'-r - y hea - r - t pre - pa-re Hi-m ro - om and

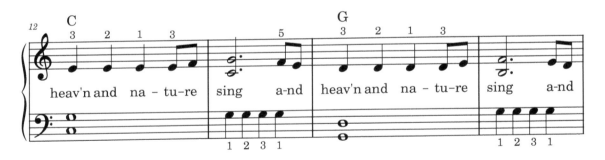

heav'n and na - tu-re sing a-nd heav'n and na - tu-re sing a-nd

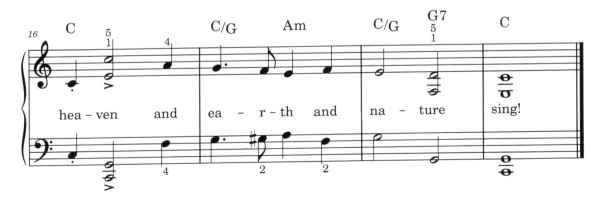

hea - ven and ea - r - th and na - ture sing!

The Holly and the Ivy

Traditional Christmas Hymn
by George Winston

Twelve Days of Christmas

Traditional Christmas Hymn

3

We Three Kings

Traditional Christmas Hymn

While Shepherds Watched Their Flocks By Night

Traditional Christmas Hymn

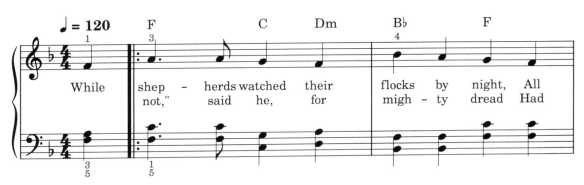

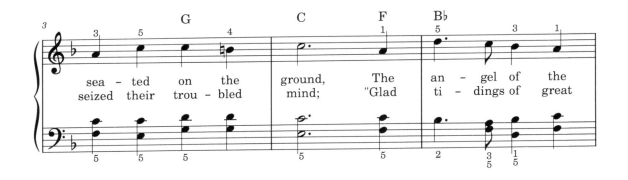

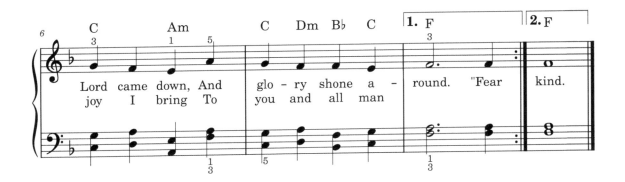

We hope you enjoyed this book and that it inspired in you a true love for music!

It would be so great if you could rate us on Amazon and leave a review, it means so much and helps us make more excellent content just like this.

APPENDIX A – CHORDS

Chords are a combination of three notes played at once with the left hand, to accompany the melody being played with the right hand.

This is a simpler way of playing music with both hands, and you can choose to play chords with your left hand instead of playing the melody In Bass Clef.

Chords are annotated by the capital letters above the music lines. Use the guide on the next page to help you understand how each chord is played.

Chords are always played one octave lower than the melody!

PIANO CHORDS

KEY	MAJOR	MINOR	SEVENTH	AUGMENTED	DIMINISHED
A					
B					
C					
D					
E					
F					
G					

Printed in the USA
CPSIA information can be obtained
at www.ICGtesting.com
LVHW082003171123
764248LV00009B/908

9 789655 752946